And when that happens, what

whispers of the past of the

voices in the present and echoes

say good bye

can be saved in your Memory Box.

past

whispers of the past of the past

treasured forever in your heart

which have voices in the present and echoes in

the future it leave behind a place — say goo

t is left?

person left of the past.

Some can be saved in your Memory Box.

memories — whispers of the past of the past

All can be treasured forever in your heart.

which have voices in the present and echoes

The Memory Box

Gathering the Keepsakes of the Heart

by Mary Kay Shanley
Illustrations by Paul Micich

To my mother, Irene, and to my children Shanley, Jason and Amy.
Both generations have given me so much. —MKS

To Amy, my grandmother, who once lived in a sod hut. She gave me a wooden box
and much more. To my grandfather, Torrence, who rode horses on the open prairie
and played baseball until the light was gone. —PM

Special thanks to Carolyn Hart Bryant and Alice B. Acheson, whose marvelous
editing was eclipsed only by their confidence that, truly, there was a beautiful
story among all those words. And thanks, also, to our friend Malinda.

Published by Sta-Kris, Inc., P.O. Box 1131, Marshalltown, Iowa 50158
Printed and bound in the Republic of Korea
Printed by Dong-A Publishing and Printing Co., Ltd.
ISBN 1-882835-32-8
The illustrations in this book were rendered in alkyd on linen.
The text was set in Linotype Hiroshige medium and bold.
Calligraphy by Sally Cooper Smith
Photos by D.E. Smith
Leaf and Snowflake by Ari Micich
Designed by Sally Cooper Smith and Paul Micich

———◦◦◦◦———

Each of us must leave behind a place — say goodbye
to a person — let go of the past.

And when that happens, what is left?
Memories — whispers of the past
which have voices in the present
and echoes in the future.

Some can be saved in your Memory Box.

All can be treasured forever in your heart.

———◦◦◦◦———

It was autumn and the last time we would drive up to the house.

The movers would arrive later in the day to take
my mother's furniture to her new apartment in the city.

Away from the home she had known for 40 years — almost half of her life.
A home with stairs she was now too tired to climb. Rooms too numerous
for only one person. A yard too big to enjoy and flowers too overgrown to tend.

Away from the home where I had grown up.
A home with dormer windows across from my bed and
a basement where I played with dolls for hours on end.
A lawn on which I could still stand, barefooted, *and feel
my roots reaching deep into the foundations of my life.*

Away from the home my daughter had visited each summer.
A haven of simple rituals: walking to the library, riding to the
cemetery with her Grandma to water the geraniums, eating pizza
at Leon's, sitting on the green bench by the garage listening to the
evening and sharing secrets.

I did not want the movers to come.

"I have some special things in this old hat box," my mother called from her bedroom. "Please put it in the car right now. Otherwise, I just know it will end up on that big truck."

Her impatience was uncharacteristic, my response distracted. "Okay. In a minute. I'll add it to my list. I've got a list here somewhere."

I wondered if I'd get everything done. And I worried that I wouldn't get anything done. The day seemed so hollow. I felt so aimless.

Then my daughter called to me. "Come up here, Mom!
You've got to see this old wooden box I found in the attic. Somebody
must have made it just for you because your name's carved inside the lid,
and there are lots of cool things in it!"

"Maybe later," I replied with a very audible sigh. "There's just too much
that has to be done right now."

An oven to clean. A phone to disconnect. Picture hangers to pull out of the walls.
A few things still to pitch.

Too many loose ends.

Too much to forget when all I wanted to do was remember.

It was sometime later before I realized how quiet
the house had become.

I'd been in the fruit cellar, trying to decide what to do with the empty Mason jars. Give them away? Pack them? Finally, I went upstairs for another cup of coffee. There was nobody in the kitchen or living room. I stopped at the foot of the stairs and heard voices coming from my old bedroom.

The two of them were sitting side by side on the edge of the mattress, and resting on my daughter's lap was the old wooden box she'd found in the attic.

"Grandma says Grandpa made this box for you when you were little," my daughter announced.

I smiled. **"Your Grandpa said it was a place to keep my memories. My 'treasures,' he called them. He said everyone should have a treasure box of some kind."**

"For real treasures?" She was giving me one of those I-doubt-it looks.

"Well, they're treasures to me. Things I wanted to save for one reason or another," I replied.

The box had been fashioned of pine salvaged from the
house where my father had grown up. He had sanded the
wood, then stained and rubbed it with oil. The shadowbox
lid, about half an inch deep, hid the box's only hardware —
brass hinges — when closed. A handmade diamond in the
center of the lid had been cut from thin pieces of walnut and
maple, then inlaid and surrounded by a thin strip of maple.

"Can we go through the box, Mom?" my daughter asked. **"Please?"**

But there was no time to look at treasures now. No time for memory sharing or
storytelling. The movers were coming. I carried the wooden box outside and put it
in the trunk of my car, next to my mother's hat box.

Just before we left the house for the last time,
I borrowed the neighbor's spade to dig up one of
my mother's peony plants. *And with each inch that
the spade went deeper into the ground, I could feel
my roots being loosened from their foundations.*

Autumn continued. Time to dig up the cannas and tuberous begonias in our flower bed, to mulch the strawberry patch and clear last summer's tomato plants from the vegetable garden. Time to plant one more bunch of tulip bulbs.

Time to stick my mother's peony plant in new ground.

But late at night, I would find myself wondering whether the new people living in my mother's house were tending the garden with the same care that we had for so many years.

Winter gradually nudged its way in. As had become her habit in recent winters, my mother tended to stay indoors, and my daughter began spending the better part of each Saturday visiting her Grandma in the new apartment in the city.

On one particularly snowy afternoon, my daughter begged me to come along as well. "Please, Mom. Remember the hat box that Grandma didn't want the movers to pack? She put it in a closet in her apartment and forgot where it was until this week. She promised we could go through it today. Aren't you curious what's in that box?"

I shook my head, declining the invitation. No, there was too much housework to do. Bills to pay. Errands to run. Mail to answer.

So only my mother and daughter spent that snowy Saturday examining the precious contents of Grandma's old hat box.

That evening, my daughter chattered all the way through supper, telling us about the delights they'd found...

"There were bunches of photos. Pictures of Grandma in school plays and Grandma with her girlfriends. Did you know that they had to wear black dresses back then? Hers had puffy sleeves and really long skirts. And Grandma's hair was so dark and wavy. She was really pretty, wasn't she, Mom?"

"She still is, don't you think?" I replied.

My daughter nodded, then went on. "And there were record books — that's what Grandma called them — from when she was a teacher in a one-room schoolhouse. It was just like the schools we read about in history. All these kids in different grades, studying different subjects. And Grandma was the only teacher so she had to spend lots of time keeping track of who knew what..."

She paused for a breath and I slipped in a comment. "I've seen those record books. I used to play teacher and keep records just like hers."

"Cool, Mom," she replied. "And did you ever see the rose from Grandpa's funeral? Grandma keeps it inside a little piece of waxed paper that's folded into a square and paper-clipped shut. Grandma said the rose used to be red, but now it's brown and kind of flaky."

Yes, I thought to myself. I remember the rose.
I kept another one for myself.

"The last thing Grandma took out of her hat box was a silver lion bank Grandpa got when he was little. He told Grandma that he only had one penny to put in it. So one day when his big brother was gone, he took some of his pennies off the dresser and put them in, too."

"Are you making this up?" I interrupted my daughter. I'd seen the bank before, but never heard this story, never thought taking another person's money was something my father would have done.

"Mom, please. I'm not finished! His brother never said anything, but it always bothered Grandpa, so the first time he made his own money, he told his brother what he'd done and gave him the pennies back. And then Grandpa cried.

"Grandma said the only other time he ever cried was the day you were born, Mom."

Instantly, I felt a strange mixture of love and loss churning inside me. And I wished, with all my heart, that I had found time to share that snowy Saturday with my mother and my daughter.

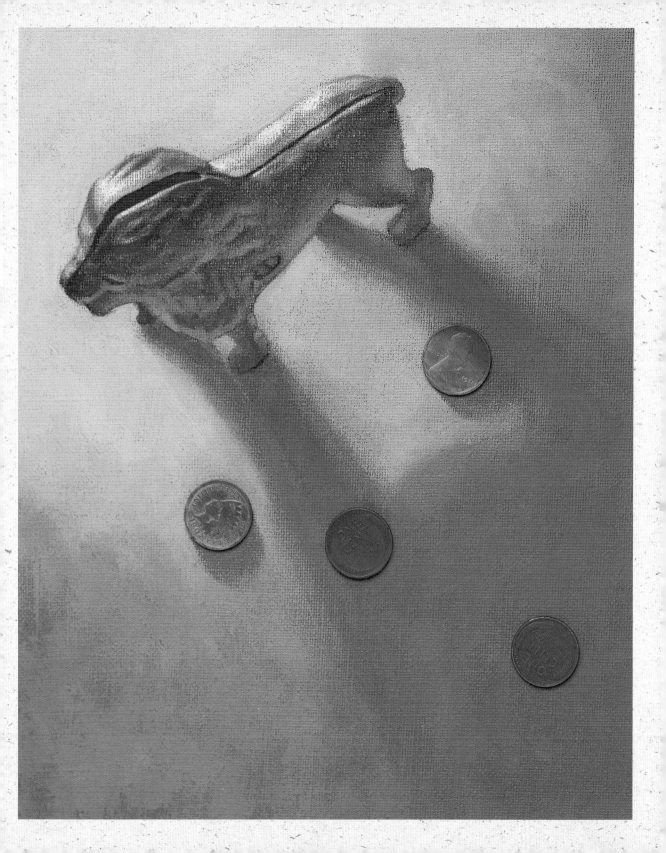

At last the snow melted, and the
sun began to warm the earth.
It was still too early to garden, but
never too early to dream. So I
invited my mother over to wander
through the seed catalogs.

Just before she arrived, I was
rummaging around for spring
jackets when I came across my
Memory Box.

"You'll never guess what I found," I said
when my mother arrived. "That Memory Box!
I'd put it away on a shelf the day you
moved, but...."

She laughed. "But you FORGOT where
it was. Right?"

Well, yes. "It might be fun to go through it,"
I suggested. "But we'd better get your grand-
daughter in here. She'd never forgive us
otherwise!"

So the three of us spent the
evening pulling treasures from
my Memory Box—

My favorite cloth baby book, "The ABCs"

A tassel from college graduation

An old wooden spoon

"Look, Mom. It's all slanted on one side…"

"I know," I replied. "Wooden spoons get that way when they've been used over a hot stove for years. This belonged to my favorite aunt…"

My mother leaned forward to touch the spoon. "I always knew she was your favorite aunt," she said.

"Well, every time I picture her, she's cooking. In her kitchen, wearing one of those aprons that you slip your arms through and tie in the back. She was always stirring something on the stove with that spoon. I used to stand on a chair next to her, ready to taste."

A tiny replica of the U.S. Capitol from our senior class trip

A funeral card from a friend who died too young

My cocker spaniel's leather collar, cracked with age

"Your mother and that dog —Shawnee — grew up together," Grandma said.
"Your mother would come home from school every afternoon and walk
Shawnee around the block. They'd always go down the driveway and turn
north. Never south."

Remembering Shawnee made me smile. "I'd throw an old shoe and
he'd race after it, but he wouldn't give it back until he was ready," I said.
"And when I was sad, we'd sit on the green bench by the garage.
Side by side. For as long as I wanted."

A candle from Confirmation

A ticket stub from the first movie I saw with the man I would marry

An unopened packet of radish seeds

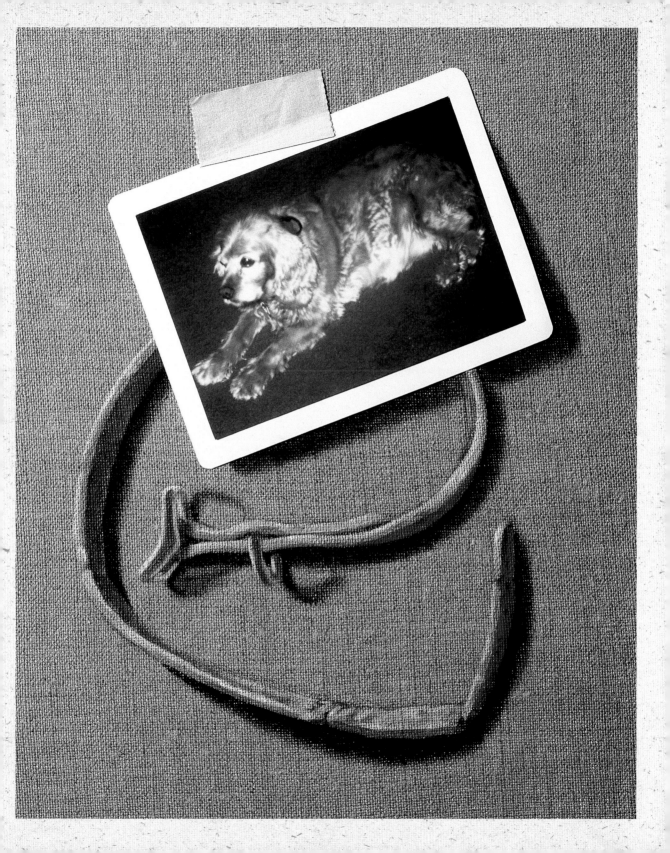

"What's this? my daughter asked, peering at the yellowed paper that still clearly bore the instructions to "plant in rows 18 inches apart."

"Let me guess!" my mother said first. "It's from Mr. Hayes! Am I right?"

I had to laugh. "Yes!" I turned to my daughter. "He was a marvelous old man who lived next door when I was growing up. I always helped him plant a garden in the spring. First, he'd break up the dirt clods, then turn the hoe sideways to open up long, straight rows. Finally, I'd kneel down and drop the seeds in because I 'bent easier.'"

"The radishes were always ready first. So I'd pull them and we'd clean them and put bunches in baskets to give away. He said giving vegetables away was the best part of gardening."

Eventually, the box was empty, but I felt curiously full. Leaning back into the sofa, I allowed myself to relish a kinship with my past that, for some reason, I had feared was gone.

It was my daughter who broke the silence. "I've got something I want to show you," she announced. "I'll be right back."

She returned with a shoe box tucked under one arm. She sat down and held out a bookmark bordered in pale blue lace. In its center, a large diamond, made up of nine smaller diamond sections, had been cross-stitched with blue and white embroidery floss.

"Grandma, you helped me stitch this when I stayed at your house one summer. Remember? I made mistakes all the time, but you'd get me back on track. See? These X's aren't really supposed to be here."

She pointed to a section where she'd gotten off by one square a couple of times.

"I told her that didn't matter," my mother said. "After all, no two diamonds are alike. And these diamonds are extra special because they're handmade. Just like the diamond on the lid of the Memory Box."

"That's what made me think of this bookmark," my daughter replied. "I'm going to start my very own Memory Box with this bookmark. That way, when I'm all grown up, I'll still remember those summers at your house, Grandma."

And with that, she carefully laid her bookmark in the empty shoe box.

Green once again covered the drab brown of winter. Lilacs perfumed the air, and clumps of tulips and daffodils swayed to spring's warm breezes. Already, seed potatoes had been entrusted to the rich, black soil. Everywhere, new growth peeked out amidst the remnants of last year's flowers and plants.

My mother often joined us for Sunday dinner. Afterward, we'd take a leisurely stroll through the yard. When we could talk her into it, my daughter would come along, to listen to us name plants, recall where each tree and bush came from, and see what hadn't survived the winter.

And in the lateness of this particular afternoon, it was my mother who slowly knelt down and touched, ever so gently, a clump of reddish shoots that were pushing their way up toward the sun. **"That was my peony plant,"** she said simply. Then she smiled. **"Now, it's yours."**

I stood very still, looking down at the new growth. *And slowly, that marvelous feeling of my own roots reaching deep into the foundations of my life began to wash over me once again.*

But on this day, there was a difference. Because finally and for the first time, I understood that my foundations — like my memories — were not harbored in a particular place.

> Not in a certain house
> Not in a favorite aunt's kitchen
> Not in a special small town
> > Nor in a wooden box

We walked back indoors: my mother on one side, my daughter on the other.

As time passes, do our memories get left behind
in empty rooms and gardens left untended?
Or can we carry them with us and transplant
them in the rich soil of a new life
to bear new blossoms?

As time passes, do our memories

get left behind in empty rooms and

gardens left untended?

As time passes, a

Or can we carry them with

get left ben

transport them in the rich soil

life to bear new blossoms

gardens left

As time passes, do our memori

get left behind in empty rooms and

gardens left untended?

Or can we carry them with us and